Thin Glass

Christine Degenaars

Fernwood
PRESS

Thin Glass
©2025 by Christine Degenaars

Fernwood Press
Newberg, Oregon
www.fernwoodpress.com

All rights reserved. No part may be reproduced
for any commercial purpose by any method without
permission in writing from the copyright holder.

Printed in the United States of America

Page design: Mareesa Fawver Moss
Cover design: Eric Muhr
Cover art: Sven Godec on Unsplash
Author photo: Emily Belic

ISBN 978-1-59498-179-1

*For David, Isabelle, and Emerson
and for my parents and my brother*

"I love beginnings. I honor that lit window which is there and not there."

—Charles Simic

Contents

Stepping Out of Angel's Share in Late July 10
After an Argument, I Spend
    the Evening Looking Out 12
First Son 14
The Angler's Shadow 16
Readying 18
On the Balcony, the Moon Scatters
    Such a Pretty Light 20
The Affair, Act I 21
Year I've Almost Forgotten 22
Changing in the Window 23
First Farewell 26
The Affair, Act II 28
A Knot that Holds 30
Swimmers in the Caribbean 32
a song 34
In Fall I Fear My Mother Gone 35
The Lifeguards 37
The Affair, Act III 39
On the Balcony 41

First Daughter 42
Missing My Mother in Jersey, 22 Miles Away 44
A Scenario Where I'm That Girl on Facebook................. 46
The Affair, Act IV 48
Like All Permanent Things.. 50
In the Wall I Began a Window 51
The Contractor 53
Mother's Dilemma... 55
Fisherman's Daughter... 57
The Affair, Act V... 59
No Frost on the Cars, Not Yet 61
The Ring... 63
A Woman Eats a Slice of Pizza... 65
No Bridge and the Sun Going Down 67
Vigil... 69
The Dive Pool 71
Piano... 74

Acknowledgments 77

Stepping Out of Angel's Share in Late July

Once again, I'm done up
        in a good-time-girl attitude, and there's a man

who's walking past, saying: how can I talk
        to any female, they don't understand.
I want to grab his belt loop,

pull him by my index finger, curved

as if holding a trigger, and I want
        to hold it there, just long enough

for him to see what good comes
        from letting someone know you like that.
He smells like clover. Oranges. Peach skin.

Suddenly I'm back in it, and he isn't him, and I'm

saying every single thing, but you don't need to get me
        like that. I keep telling him that if

I keep telling him about the under-
        the-bed parts of my mind maybe he'll look at things
the way they look at me. But what does that matter?

Sometimes I'm meaning so much there's no room

for anything else. What word is there for when I look
        through a window and can't tell what's me?

Let's step back. Let's talk about heat waves,

red wine, and summer time, all the things I thought
        couldn't touch me that May through August.

Let's talk about how once I lived with a man

who wasn't mine, and when he walked out
    of a cab, I wanted him

the whole way down the street.

    He was all apricots and sweet marmalade,
and when he drank he said he loved

his wife and what's left of him I didn't need.

And now—now I can't even remember his face. Am I
    making myself clear—all I mean is that people get lost

in my memories of them, and they lose

    all their skin. Undress me. I'm asking
take off your filth. Know me through seconds,

through too much blue pep—scream to me over the things

I'm telling you. Imagine what it is like now, for me, to look
    for you. At this hour, every bar smells like a name,

and every East Village neon sign keeps repeating

    there is so much more music in the things we can't own,
and I, I am an I that is exploding with song

    even if everything else stings. I am the only thing

that keeps me holy. I am the only thing that keeps me
    holy when God—

when God won't talk to a woman and wonders how.

After an Argument, I Spend
the Evening Looking Out

After all the things we've said, there's this:
a dark street on a dark night, truck
        idle on the side of the road
        below Bleecker. Taillights flare

like a pair of burners, coils hot at the back
of a stove. A woman walks by carrying
        an umbrella. It's too late
        for anything good

to happen. She crosses the street,
and my eye lingers. White dashes
        saddle the middle of the road
        like driftwood on a deep lake.

The stores, shuttered—it's a silver art,
this act of evasion. What takes the place of
        what we lack. Windows
        of the apartment building

I face are dark except a single square, bright,
hypothermic blue. There, the TV blazes
        while a couple sleeps, stretched out
        on a Murphy bed. The man's right

hand rests on the woman's right hip.
I don't mean to watch them, but I do.
        I'm looking for signs
        of life. So late at night,

how could I even be sure it happened—
whose fault then? Outside, that woman's
    walking, I follow her doll's hand
    as it rises up like a single

piece of flint. She hails a cab, gives
her jacket a swift shake, steps in.
    One moment, she's swallowed
    by the car's backseat. Then both, gone.

First Son

Last night Jake said
we could disappear any second,

just say the word, having outgrown
this one bedroom, this lack.

How can I picture anything outside myself
in a week's time, I'm not ready.

I want a Thursday night, tight sequined skirt,
tugging it down my thigh on the subway.

A stranger to see the real thing under
my skin, whole of my twenties

laid bare and repeated again,
one long carnival ride after another,

mango sunset, cotton candy smell,
winking lights turned music, dancing across

a wide mirror, baby teeth sharp, black
along the gum, my bare feet, cracked glass—

I don't feel good. The children next door shriek
as they take to the elevator, go down nine flights

for fresh air. Snot dried to their lips,
hands sticky as they press the button down

until it beeps. How little I want
them, how bad is that to say? My stomach grows

sore, my back aches in preparation.
I don't think I like myself enough

to make two. Motherhood: a form
of vagrancy, no body my own. Manhattan skyline

strips down, without shadow. The sidewalks blaze,
June at last. It nearly happens to me.

The Angler's Shadow

Before I was born, my father collected
feathers and fur in old coffee cans,
kept them in the shed like nails.

It was his habit, washcloth
over his shoulder, to clean and salt
what he gathered. Most mornings

he woke as scavenger, bruised
his lips in my mother's hair, and left
for the little strip of highway which ran

from our street out east and north.
He searched. The days before you,
he says, unrolled like a thin, white gap.

Only when moths gathered
at the screen door would he return,
pockets full of goose quill and fox tail

snipped from roadkill he found along
the guardrails. He always came back
dirty, formed of mud, of earth.

Sometime later, I went to watch him work,
hidden under a sheet. I wanted to see
what it was like for him to exist

without me. I wanted to witness
that gap. Scissors in his hand, bead
balanced between his teeth, the shed

glowed like a tissue box on fire.
I crept closer, invisible. Under
the brutal light, he clipped kip tail

about a nail's length, held it along
the hook's body. I watched him wrap it
in orange thread, take out his hackle.

So many colors, too many shades
of wood and tan and yellow.
He picked one, pulled the line

taut, stood back from his workbench.
Come here, little ghost, he said to me,
and I stepped to his side and looked.

Readying

Listen I say to a younger self, I know:

        this isn't how we pictured it—
deep in drugstore makeup, eyes ringed

blue, smudged black, we are the girl we were

        at the roller rink and what were we
then? Made of Black Ice air fresheners

and diet soda, nail polish chipped, then

        swallowed, we swore forever we'd stay
untamed, untouched, despite what they told us—

those hours in idling cars, the radio red-lit

        and repeating "Firework" by Katy Perry;
it was always dark—no, nothing would touch us,

nothing would creep under our skin and stick.

        But those boys, where are they now?
The ones that tempted and tuned us, attempted to

turn us into sun-blanched corkscrews—they stand

        in line at CVS, their pinkies mining
for earwax, they buy condoms and blue Listerine,

while some girl named Meg or Katie waits

        by the automatic doors and texts. Bridled,
bored, bangs pulled behind one ear, is this

what happened next? After what we wanted—

      then, didn't. Little self, pick
at the pink curve of my gums, floss out food

in the bathroom mirror. The gap between my teeth

      is a gate, a welcome mat, the only way in
or out. Come! See how the streetlights lark

in the open sky like blinking boats lost at sea.

      To turn thirty in so much space feels
extravagant. Come with me. Please, come see.

On the Balcony,
the Moon Scatters Such a Pretty Light

He wants me home, asks what it is
about four walls that makes me

so much like a bird. I don't know—
it's hard for him to love me.

Most nights I'm devoted
to the clean countertop, the folded laundry,

pans stacked neatly in the first drawer,
which is how my mother did it,

my father at the sink, washing his hands.
Here, she pulls the bobby pins from her hair.

There, he touches the pearls of her spine.
They are captive, kept, and not unhappy.

I am a sparrow. Married too, but still
my mind goes south, I search for seeds

in the frost. My husband finds me,
digging in cold grass, my jeans stained

and smelling like earth. Other times,
we listen for cars outside, and I curl into him;

he holds a mirror to me. Whatever he does,
he does to make me whole. What I'd do

to lose this need—forget the wing
at the window, the balcony begging me.

The Affair, Act I

    I am everything

my mother told me

    I would be if I wasn't

        careful.

    April again,

sweet-sick smell

    of tequila, my green coat and you:

        writer, teacher, taker of my hand,

    you walked your index and third finger up

my thigh as if journeying

    for pleasure, pillage, power.

        Might I

    never move.

Come here,

    you said, then,   no   then,

        closer,

    under the light

so I can

    see you.

Year I've Almost Forgotten

    What of this was real—I break open
that spring and—what happens? God knows.

    Seems so much of my life has narrowed
me into a long, black wire. Jake pours us a drink,

    covers the candle with a coaster. After,
I sit on our bed, stand in front of the mirror, touch

    my stomach. Still, I'm groggy
with loss. Childless too, childless maybe. He sleeps,

    his breath like the whirr of a warming car.
Later I dream myself swollen—my baby, pink.

    I spend the dark nightmaring for a name.
Each time I find one, it slips from my mouth,

    my mouth, an empty O. Child lost in our
sheets, I wake searching the bed for your little feet.

Changing in the Window

I don't close the blinds.
        It's not that I forget,
although sometimes I do,

        it's just—if some
woman or man were to make
        the effort, frequent

antique shops along Bleecker,
        looking for the perfect
pair, binoculars strung

        with an emerald string,
and were they to hurry
        them home,

wrapped in white tissue,
        if he were to take them
down from the top cabinet,

        sneak to the open
window and sink
        to his knees,

were she to keep
        the lights off,
so I couldn't guess

        from what dark
she waited or watched,
        were they to cast

lots as to the bra
        I would choose,
which pants I'd pull

        from the bottom
drawer, if they tallied
      how often

my left leg slipped first
        into the mouth
of my jeans at six thirty

      on Monday mornings,
then let them.
      This is yearning:

the blank space in an open
      window. What makes
room for me to desire, them

      to desire me. Who'd hide
from this, the almost
      tender, who'd dare?

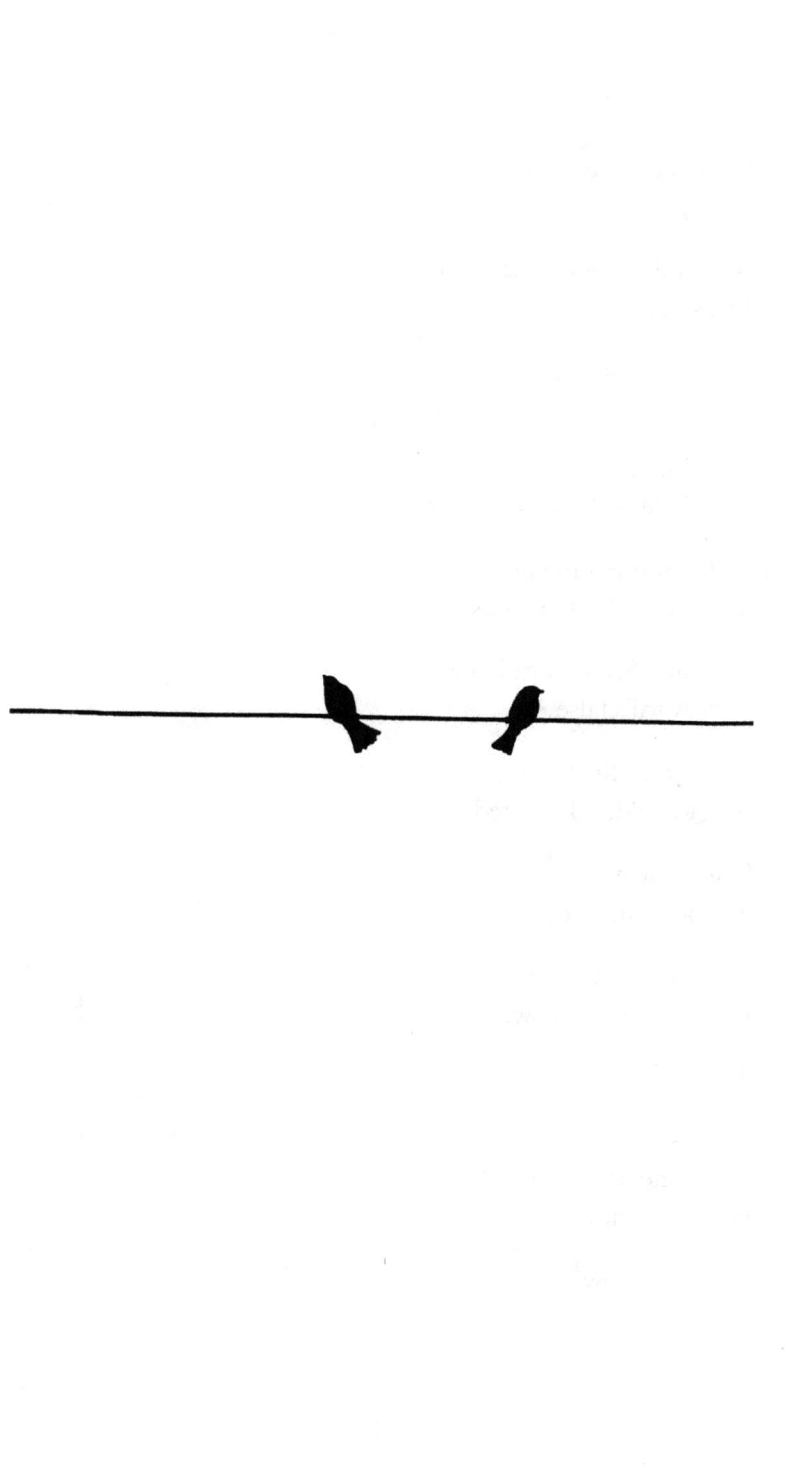

First Farewell

I am not as beautiful
as I think I am.

Remembering the last time
I was here

and a guy, now gone,
who came the way summer

songs do, rustling
my insides out of me.

Nothing turns me ugly
like a man. Walking past

Carmine Street, I'm in love
with April's false

spring and the feeling
that I could, if I wanted,

reach down
any boy's throat

and pull out what I have
waited so long to own.

There's something pretty
in burrowing

into bone, the depraved
crouching down

in the marrow
the way soldiers do,

taking cover in the glitter
of ambush. I am angry

at the sunflowers,
lingering near the traffic light,

because they're older
than me and lovely

and don't breathe foul
lipstick breath or sleep

with their mouths open
and damp. They never dream

of the bodies
they've known, stacked

like splintered driftwood,
their faces, mirrors of their own

faces, indiscriminate
and aging and blank.

The Affair, Act II

You found me,

all of twenty-three and lonely,
    a loose sequin in a bathroom sink,
        an empty ashtray,

calling my mother under the neon halo of a speakeasy.

What exists here,

between you and me,
    exists still.
        But what of the rum drum of your name

and the steam that floats up from subway grates?

Sure—there was a time

when what you made me
    made me
        feel lucky.

Wasn't it you

who asked that one, sad thing:

was I all in for playing chicken, chasing ghosts,
    leaning into the sound of loose change,
        clinking,

and you, could I make you

a man I could love?

Now eight years of remembering
    the manhole cover,
        its mouth open like an almost-

scream, I still don't know the answer.

A Knot that Holds

It was different when we bait-fished.
We'd keep minnows in old bottles

or plastic bags, always with enough
water. It was my father's justice: never

hurt something until you were ready
to kill it, then do it fast. When we needed one,

we'd pour the bottle out, a slow dribble, until
a tail or head appeared, or we'd scoop our hands

into the creel, spilling water everywhere,
wait for the slick, jittered body

to swim into the caves of our fists.
It wasn't cruel to sew the needle through

their mouths, down the length of their spines
and hook them, as long as we filled the water

again, enough for the rest of the bait
to breathe. Once, I left the bottle empty,

kept it on a stone in the sun and waded
into the stream.

My father found it, bait buoyed belly up.
He poured them out onto the grass

for the crane and crow, he would not
speak. That whole day I wandered

between the bank, watching my father,
and the car. I sat in the open trunk, dangled

the tips of my boots in the gravel,
drew figure eights. I waited, wanted

to right that wound and go home. Shame
is a braided line. It ties what I've done to me.

Swimmers in the Caribbean

After a line by Susan Mitchell

At a Starbucks
on Union Avenue, it rains,
and a stranger closes his eyes

over me. I'd like to blame
him for this, how much
I am like a window now—

it was a cab ride,
those early years. We drove
to Central Park, you pressed

a piece of cloth to a cut
on my heel, remember? Like oil,
it shined in the car light.

Come with me
to Trinidad and Tobago
you said. Your wife,

your girls gone. Port of Spain,
the air salted with spring—there
you said the lime goes on

forever. I saw us—
beach hat and folding chairs,
watch the ocean tag the shore,

retreat. Ships in the bay
bobbing like bucking horses,
towels the color of sunset.

You said at night we'd sit
flushed with rum and cheap wine,
side by side on the balcony,

looking out—darkness
like the hem of a sheer skirt.
You in white

linen and well into forty.
My mother warned me:
never love a man

you can't understand.
Your teeth were a fence
painted between

your lips. I shouldn't
have believed you.
Sometimes still, sometimes—

love is a dark pool
at the bottom of a dark well or
something else: refuse

and rainwater
which take me back home.
What I say, I say without

mercy, and what you said,
listen to me—
they were not songs.

a song

her mouth was like rain on hot
pavement; her body trebled
with fervid frequency; she
poured out sound so near your own
name and did without trying;
she loved the men who looked
for her, loves the ones who didn't,
their lips, lined up like unstemmed
minims, she threaded them when
the moon's lap was full of Venus;
then that once she let a smile
loose without looking up—
remember it, it was still
only the start of October.

In Fall I Fear My Mother Gone

The hard thing is to say it
slow. I've tried, counted the birds
weary along the power line,

each a small barrette. Soft rain,
I'm empty without it. Kitchen
windows blink back at me, dark.

Counters wane, wiped clean.
Today is over, and my daughter,
if she exists, sleeps.

We keep the door open,
hallway lights on—no matter
where I am, I hear her.

October, crisp and orange, shade
of someone leaving. How real things are
once we say them. I take a nectarine

to the porch, a can of seltzer. This
is living. The railing wraps around
the stairs, each pillar a woman.

She keeps the top bar from
crashing to the bottom. Tension—
brings peace. Second autumn missing,

and still it's like she's out for coffee,
getting the mail, my daughter
skipping after her shadow

like a loose thread—how close am I
to breaking? This evening, empty space
takes a physical form. The fog is milkweed

cracked open. It separates me from
everything else: the yard, car, need,
my mother, I need her. It's stuck in me.

The Lifeguards

We watched them come to shore still shining
with fish scales and open water.

We wanted to touch them. It wasn't desire
exactly but something closer

to what Thomas must have felt, passing
his fingers through the hands of Christ,

a disbelief turned electric.
Our reality was that something had

happened, and it was being performed.
Never did we see the moment

of rescue, but once two carried
a rowboat into the breakers, the oars

bounced as if fanning smoke. We ran
to the little hem of shoreline, watched

the men jump into each wave, practicing.
Each time they ducked in the white foam,

we held our breath to see if we, too,
were holy. When they were past the waves

where the water turned a dark green,
my mother cupped a shell to my ear—*here,*

listen for their sound. I held my breath
longer. Even now, I believe the sacred begins

with something shared, and so I shared
this with them, their deep breaths, heavy

breathing, wet mouths open, holding
then letting go, the exhaustion. If ever

asked, I could say I'd seen God,
and my body remembered.

The Affair, Act III

I was sin
            and you.

Not that long riddle of stairs to your office,
        the dark room,
               how convincing you were

in dim lighting.

On the floor, we sat cross-legged,
               spun a bottle

like kids
        in an empty shed.

                    I'll kiss you

on the industrial carpet. You say:
        I will devour you—

    and after

you will come back to me   always.

    Your wife,   you loved her, said

love was her

               cupped hand at your chin,

        held as if
           to catch rain—   and me.

Me,   you said,   I was carved from you—

no,   you and I   had sprung

                from some same thing.

It's not bad, you said.

One sin,

we did it twice.

On the Balcony

When we were sleeping, nearly sleeping, and
I was on my side and husband, you, with your right
    hand, claimed the slope of my thigh,
    valley of hip and bone, when we looked out
the window at other windows, and when we closed
our eyes, then opened again, to measure the faint
    ongoings and coming backs, the evening pace
    of peace, that silky wing, as we slipped to sleep,
a light turned on, someone surfaced on the balcony,
faced us, lit a cigarette and spit off the ribboned railing
    that looked like the toothy black of piano keys,
    and yes, I said, he sees us—his eyes on me,
our resting form, he knows I'm watching still—still
we didn't close the blinds, not you nor me, we let him
    in, and something was lost, washed clean and
    tossed to him from us, from me, and that night
it was that faceless face I dreamed, and we, I
dreamed, were tigers, we paced an empty cage.

First Daughter

A scenario: something
tragic happens to my family, all my friends,

and I go off alone to settle again into a bright
sadness. In this, I have a daughter.

We live above a bakery,
sleep on cots of newspaper, old cloth;

my hands raw from the bread and scones
I knead each morning. With cupcake liners,

my daughter makes skirts for her fingers,
we never have enough for her pinkies.

Still she twirls, hands up. In the single shaft
of light, dust turns the air a kind of gold. Otherwise,

we stay in shaded cabins, soggy with pine,
hers a slightly smaller version of mine.

We carve our names into mossy stones,
sound out the letters, "klee" then "ree."

Soil collects like a dark stream under our nails.
We wake groggy, wet with dew, hair

matted like deer or wild boar. I chase her
on my hands and knees, and she runs, skips

over an open root and becomes fully fawn.
But sometimes, I imagine my girl, and she's nothing

more than human. We sit on dirty benches
in airport terminals, her hand in mine,

head resting on our luggage.
We argue to show my patience. She laughs

to demonstrate my good humor
in calamity. I carry her door to door,

day to day, as I would an old suitcase.
I open, lay her bare. I would, I do.

Missing My Mother in Jersey, 22 Miles Away

Cold November wind,
I beg you—

bring whatever it is
I've been looking for

back to me: my hairbrush,
pair of lost shoes, the keys,

my mother. I'm entering
a world of words like *silent*

will that I wear as a type of jacket.
Everything these days it seems

is quietly tugging, prying things
true, pushing the inevitable

to show itself in rhinestone
and faux leather. I'm moving

what I want forward, making it
real for money, a promotion

or because I want it and, well,
I am most myself living in this state

of yearning. This morning
a plastic bag rolled, open-mouthed

across the street, a city's turn
at tumbleweed. I'm preparing

to need her when she isn't here.
I'm working through a kind

of preemptive mourning
as I make coffee, step in

the shower. On Facebook, a girl
I know wrote the worst thing

about the death of her mother
was that she didn't have anyone

to ask if a bowl was microwave safe.
She said she still picks up

the phone sometimes, rings
the empty number, waits.

A Scenario Where I'm That Girl on Facebook

I'm standing on a bridge
in Bradley Beach counting to three.
This is the second life, the one

I left someplace to live. Unbearable
sometimes, winters here are cold
despite what they tell you, the land: flat

that they got right.
Most days I descend the stairs,
pace the lawn. Across the street

the neighbor's sprinklers run all night,
the sidewalk's never dry. Weeds sprout
from grout, unwieldy as hairs,

and I can't stop seeing you. Bedhead
in the kitchen, reading the paper,
the round table stained with print.

To sit there, coffee blooming
into that familiar smell, my daughter
on your lap, making sailor hats

from the sports section—Mom
I just want to call. Receive a letter,
carrier pigeon, little scroll tied

to his heel, anything that tells me
it isn't over, you're still here.
Today Cleary and I dragged

that old table to the curb, the crack
down the middle nearly split us
in two. If only I could call—

it's been just over a year.
Out here, I can only see you
as living. I still can't say the words.

The Affair, Act IV

Whether it was

        those birds,

        sinking to shadow,

or too much Patron,

          we came to a bar on the corner,

        where we could play

        husband and wife,

      trade napkins, write lines

one at a time

      to one another.

The April blooms,

      then you,

      then again,

again, until I no longer knew   which of us   was me.

            Whatever we were,

              I wanted it,

      wrote my wanting,

      you wrote

      it made you

          mine—   well,

even when you were,

                  you know,

                  you weren't.

Like All Permanent Things

he says this one will only last
a little while. I was that bird we saw

years ago, when we left for church,
the one in the glue trap, our mother

wouldn't let us touch because it was
raining and dirty, and for once couldn't we

just be somewhere on time.
On this park bench, head between my knees,

I feel the way we found him, a little heap.
It's morning somewhere, my brother says,

and in that place, there's a bridge,
warm with sun. Picture it, count to ten.

Later, my window open to the street,
it happens, that sparrow—stuck

behind my teeth. Each time,
I open my mouth, a fluttered wing,

my tongue like an earthworm
it plucks out of me.

In the Wall I Began a Window

    built to jump through.
For months, I deconstructed crates,

stacked wood in the freezer

    for safekeeping. This was all
        until, like killed deer,

    I carried them down to the rug,
saw and drill bit heavy in my hands.

Against the door, my shadow heaved

    like a mountain growing
        under heavy snow.

    My pets followed. Birds dove
for my eyes, the giraffe hid under the table,

her long neck threaded through the chairs

    like yellow rope. The elephant turned,
        he couldn't watch,

    his trunk traced his outline
on the floor so he wouldn't forget what we

were leaving. I slit each strip of plywood

    into four pieces, everything needed
        to measure 37 ¼. Listen,

    I said to my animals,
glass is the hardest part (by-product of ironwork

mix of soda ash and sand, dust, stone, dust).

   I flaunted this—what I could make
     to set us free.

  Suddenly, the outside appeared—
and it looked so much like the inside to me,

but I hungered, and my animals hungered,

    and we gathered everything up,
      went running for the open

   space—leapt—suspended—we
bounced back, fell, reflected.

Instead of a window, I'd built

   a mirror, that other kind of glass.

The Contractor

For two days now, a man in a motorcycle vest

        busies in my neighbor's apartment. Sometimes

he's in the kitchen, opens, bends, buries his head

        in the dishwasher, runs his palm across the top

cabinets. Other times, he just tugs the freezer handle,

        washes down the windows, stands on the balcony

smoking a cigarette.

        He's the only one who's seen me.

He doesn't wave or smile, raise his left or right

        eyebrow, grant a nod of recognition—no.

But when I get up and step to the thin glass

        that separates me

from everything else, when I look down sixteen flights

        to remind myself: when I feel most alive, I am

my closest—he sees me the way I see him,

        a kind of open looking, an inability to look

away. Our distance is formidable. There's my whole room,

        then the window, gap of air between my place

and the balcony, the balcony itself, another window,

        him. It's far enough that we can stare

and pretend we go unnoticed. But I notice,

    change in the bathroom, think about closing

the blinds so my husband, his hair peeking

        from the top sheet, can keep his dreams

private. Will I break our peace, our one and two-ness,

    for this chance to witness—

Mother's Dilemma

I come home with a candle tucked
in my purse. Jake's in the kitchen,

he looks up. I say, all this might be worse
with a daughter. SoHo, where I just was,

is so crowded with money, there'd be
no place for empty bottles, a stray sock,

which I know my baby, whoever she is,
would slip from her little foot, leave discarded

on a subway grate. Would a passing train
raise it up like an autumn leaf—would we

find it? Is this what we want:
a daughter gamboling between

sport coats, stiff-tongued shoes, caverned
and clacking; for her to treat men

like rocks on a jetty—don't slip, step
around them, say excuse me—always

both a part and apart from them?
Is there a love we couldn't have

without her? We talk, watch the news,
light the candle. Everything flickers cobalt

or gold against the long stretch of blank wall.
He rests his head on my stomach,

listens for active limbs, that eager,
kicking foot. There's nothing in me now

or yet. We haven't decided. Yet
still, I sting for something as I lie

beside him. What it is, we are
too tired to dream.

Fisherman's Daughter

Oswego: the trout there are monsters,
known to eat mice and newborns,

they prey upon shadows cast
across open water, come to the surface only

to pull you in. They see you
before seeing you, my father warned.

Once around Christmas, he left us
to stand in the middle of the lake,

suspended. He fished through the December
night. Long johns, down coat, wool hat,

boots with metal grips—it was as if
he stepped into a second body

made of dried scales and leather.
This is how my father became a fish.

Just as dawn crept across the horizon,
painting my father and the sky pink

at the edges, he says she came. First as a tap-tug
then pulled—yanked—dragged him down and

under the ice, ran him from one edge of the lake
to the other. Holding his breath, submerged,

he lost his hat, the ring on his left hand,
and swam through the dark, hauling

that fish behind him. My father returned
to the surface, stung back to life.

He held the flashlight between
his teeth to prove the fish was there, his.

He couldn't stop looking.
How could anyone want to go home

after something like that? I understand.
It happened like this, in varying degrees,

each time he left our little house for the dark
water. I'd sit by the window and practice

holding my breath so that if he ever took me,
I could live under the ice with him.

The Affair, Act V

And after,
the sun just brimming,
was a papercut
    in the sky.

                      You sang
                      Michael Jackson
                      to the taxi cabs.
                      They drifted silent
                          as swans.

My mother said:
no man with a wife
and another
can be honest
    twice.

                      Maybe you loved me
                        and maybe not.

          Sometimes
          your wife rang
          as if calling me home
              for dinner.

                          I'll carry her always.

Confession:
I wanted you to say

                we were never ours
                for keeping.

But even that
is extinguished now,
        empty.

                Little coffee stain of my soul,
                I fluttered, flattered

by the birds
you blew in my eyes.

           It's not bad—
           and I believed you—

No Frost on the Cars, Not Yet

Jake warms the Jeep. It's December,
hail flicks the parking lot in cracked beads,
and still I am a question unanswered, a woman

unmoored. He thinks I'll make good as a mother
as if every wrong thing I've let into my life
does not trail me like light through the trees.

Perhaps she'll have my guilt, my tendency
to stay out too late, drink too much, want
after men that don't belong to me, who take

shots and drink beers in bars at night. Perhaps,
eager and searching, she'll cling to their whispers,
hear for her name. Perhaps she just won't love me,

and what then? One winter, years and years from now,
she might stumble out of some foreign place,
look up at the sky and mistake streetlights for stars,

her head haloed, a shadow in plowed snow.
What will she wish for—what does she want
as she stubs out her cigarette, wanders back inside.

The Ring

They call it lapping, the sound
of the lake in my window

but it's my father wearing his heavy
boots again.

Upstate New York,
where the vein of the Esopus weaves

from Winnisook to the Ashokan,
through some magic of modern piping, finds itself

in Manhattan, a water glass,
where ice cubes tink at the surface

and remind someone of the Titanic.
My father and I don waders,

lean against the open trunk of a '98 Jeep Cherokee
and ready to fish.

I'm an age not worth mentioning.
Seems everything that happens early on

happens to someone else anyway.
I'm old enough

to carry my rod *tip up* as my father calls it,
through the trees, down the bank and across.

I find slow water.
He fishes the rocks and I can hear him

wading through the muck, humming
Bob Seger *light of the moon, to a 50s tune*. Still

he says it makes him think of me, a daughter playing
by the rules.

We only keep brown trout, stock fish.
Rainbow, which are native here, are beautiful—wild.

They'll snap your line if you let them
and they taste like the river

in that fundamental way
because they're born out of it—

from the flies and larvae, intestines,
eggs and little heart that we gut

from the brown fish we keep—
and that, my father says, tastes like shit.

I can't say if we catch our limit
but when the day casts its last sun on us,

and the back of my father's neck
is red leather, we cross the stream again,

buy pretzels from the German woman in town—stale.
Always, my father says, it's the same.

Twilight's high blue ribbons the windshield
and I feel the river still—

its weight against my legs and that sound: nymphs
hatching off the surface, bubble of fast current, but mostly

my father,
his boots waterlogged, walking up the bank.

A Woman Eats a Slice of Pizza

After a poem by Natalie Diaz

with fork and knife,
      parmesan shaker,
and box of wet wipes.

She rocks a stroller
      in slow rhythm,
out came the sun,

dried up all the rain,
      toe of her left boot
curled around the wheel.

She runs her pinky through
      the sauce, carries it
to the corner of her mouth

and sucks. The hostage in me
      moves, dares to break
out, little prisoner, for now.

These days, I'm seasick always,
      and this woman is proof
of what fragile victory is possible,

reveals my future
      with each savory,
oil-filled bite. In slim strips

she rips the crust, holds it
      over the open carriage.
Like the mouth of a baby bird,

a small fist springs up,
        grabs, brings it back
down. Really, it's more

Leviathan than anything,
        reaching, then
returning to the briny deep.

Could this be what comes after
        fear, all these years I've spent
uncertain? Feed him again, for me.

No Bridge and the Sun Going Down

After a line by Yosa Buson

On a park bench, bottle
        of Beaujolais between us,
he answers, maybe all

we really know is what we've done
        and how we've lived with it.
I wonder if that's true. Seems everything

I've done has made a stranger of me. I want
        to prove it, count my mysteries
on his hands, take his fingers in my mouth.

I remind him of that summer, how little
        it feels like something I did.
Was I someone else then? Jake twists

a blade of grass into a ring, presses it
        into my palm. I don't know
what I'm asking for—perhaps a filling in,

the way water catches in cracked pavement
        or something else, something that
lasts. I worry—what's under his skin is his,

and no matter how much we empty
        ourselves into one another, could he
ever really be mine? A woman walks by,

her son knee-high and full speed beside her.
        He runs ahead—his coat opens
like wings. Maybe I want this boy or

> to be like this boy, who trusts what he loves
> is behind him. At the road's end,
> he reaches for her. He doesn't turn or look.

Vigil

My neighbor lights a candle in his open window,
    places it on the ledge. It must be cold
        in that small room, no heat matches

the steady breeze through the screen. I watch the flame dance,
    bend, break, bounce again like a bob bag springing back
        to life. From here, its small spindle of smoke rises

like a horse's mane mid-gallop, a trick the boys would play
    in school—run a finger through an open flame,
        see what happens. Lighter in a parking lot,

danger's contagious but no one ever got hurt,
    what they did was magic. Those boys gone—
        grown, myself too and now, perhaps, forgiven?

I love you, I say, to no one in particular—
    I'm remembering less and less. Down below,
        car lights illuminate a darkened window,

fogged with tic-tac-toe boards and initials. A couple passes,
    pauses, signs the glass like the bark of a tree.
        So someone knows, she says,

that we've been here. He kisses her and the streetlights
    charm like a string of champagne glasses.
        It wasn't all bad with that writer and me.

Here's to the pizza shop, the Starbucks, and subway entrance.
    Here's to all the ghosts I know, the shadow children
        not-yet-born that one day may find me.

Here's to Jake, those strangers, here's, I guess, to me.
How often do we come across a vigil?—
My neighbor lights a candle,

closes the window. He turns away and I do too.
Roll down the curtains, tie the tassels,
they droop like moth wings.

The Dive Pool

    Young and soaked tender,
she swims to the ladder, pulls herself up.

    I close the paper,
put away my phone—I could save her
    at any moment, if that's what's needed.

On her thigh, a temporary tattoo glistens.

    It draws eyes to her skin.
Sure, I'd get there in time, my daughter, my mirror,

    I'd save you from drowning—
and earlier, in the parking lot across the street,
    when a man looked, squinted

through your cover up and saw—

    did I save you then too?
I was there. I took your hand. We walked together.

    One day, might there be some part
of that stranger's August-hot want
    that you may want for?—

already you're starting to exist without me.

    I feel it, hate it, but
no soul is big enough for this man,

    you, and me. What if I tucked you
back inside, again strung tissue through
    our middles? How about I take this man—

the dark hairs of his knuckles, his thumbs,

    like two rusted hooks—and bury him
under the cement pool, to be found decades later,

        his fingernails, long and yellow-whorled
as an old shell—what about that? No.
        Daughter, there's nothing worse

than a hidden kind of living. You climb

        the diving board again—
and suddenly, it's a movie theater, many years ago

        and I am one of only two people there.
The floor is sticky—his hands are cold—
        you wave—

I can't protect you—you leap.

Piano

It begins—a woman practicing,
always this time of night.

She reaches for the black keys, hesitates,
looks down. These are her narrow fingers,

this, the thin gold band.
It's June again. Five years since

she stood and he stood and she said—
what did she say?—Was it

the white shoes she wore that day?
The blue? Down the road, dogs bark

themselves awake, and a truck drifts by—
mumbled thunder over gravel.

Despite all I've tried,
she thinks, I am myself. Still.

There, at the corner of Washington and Jane,
he'd asked how any two people could be

whole/together/free—what she'd have done
just then, to unzip her chest, walk out

and into him, her body like a coat, left
on a crowded train. To tie him there,

tethered to her, could she make that a kind
of freedom? So that years from then

they might sit at a table, read the paper
and be alone. It was possible,

wasn't it? She plays a song from memory now,
feels her way into the melody like a hand

behind her neck. It's familiar.
What it's called, I can't quite remember.

Acknowledgments

Many thanks to the editorial teams at the following journals, where these poems found their first homes, some with different titles and in different forms:
The Bear Review, "First Son"
Epiphany, "Readying," "Mother's Dilemma," "Vigil," "The Dive Pool," "Piano"
KGB Bar Literary Journal, "a song"
The Laurel Review, "First Farewell" (as "Outside the Grey Dog in Chelsea")
Nimrod International Journal of Prose & Poetry, "Missing My Mother in Jersey, 22 Miles Away"
Rattle, "Swimmers in the Caribbean"
River Heron Review, "Fisherman's Daughter" (as "Oswego, New York")
River Heron Review Editors' Prize Finalist, "Angler's Shadow"
Solar Journal, "On the Balcony," "First Daughter"
Tar River Poetry, "No Bridge and the Sun Going Down"
Zine, "In the Wall I Began a Window"

Thank you

I am beyond grateful for the advice, feedback, and friendship of my teachers and peers who made this book possible. I'd especially like to thank my husband, David, my first reader and best friend, as well as Jenna Breiter, Vanessa Ogle, Grayson Wolf, and my MFA cohort for their years of close attention to these poems and my many non-poems. Thank you to my mentors at CUNY Hunter: Catherine Barnett, Donna Masini, and Tom Sleigh for believing in me and in this. Lastly, thank you to John Anderson, whose Studies in Poetry class introduced me to the many ways one could discover and read a poem and whose encouragement, both during my time at Boston College and afterward, allowed me to imagine I could write one, too.